M000289335

HOLMES
READS
HOLMES

HOLMES
READS
HOLMES

REFLECTIONS ON THE REAL-LIFE LINKS BETWEEN THE JURIST & THE DETECTIVE

in the Library, in the Courtroom, and on the Battlefield

Featuring Arthur Conan Doyle's
THE ADVENTURE OF THE BLUE CARBUNCLE

Edited by
ROSS E. DAVIES *and*
M.H. HOEFLICH

TALBOT
PUBLISHING
Clark, New Jersey

Sir Arthur Conan Doyle (1859–1930).

Justice Oliver Wendell Holmes (1841–1935).

Copyright © 2020 by the authors for the respective chapters,
and by Ross E. Davies and M.H. Hoeflich for the volume as a whole.

ISBN 978-1-61619-647-9

All rights reserved. No part of this publication may be reproduced, stored in a retrieval system, or transmitted, in any form or by any means, electronic, mechanical, photocopying, recording, or otherwise, without the prior written permission of the publisher or the copyright holder or holders, except in the case of brief quotations embodied in critical reviews and certain other noncommercial uses permitted by copyright law.

TALBOT PUBLISHING
AN IMPRINT OF
The Lawbook Exchange, Ltd.
33 Terminal Avenue
Clark, New Jersey 07066-1321

*Please see our website for a selection of our other publications
and fine facsimile reprints of classic works of legal history:*
www.lawbookexchange.com

Library of Congress Cataloging-in-Publication Data

Names: Davies, Ross E., editor. | Hoeflich, Michael H., editor.
Title: Holmes reads Holmes : reflections on the real-life links between the
  jurist & the detective in the library, in the courtroom, and on the
  battlefield : featuring Arthur Conan Doyle's The Adventure of the Blue
  Carbuncle / edited by Ross E. Davies & M.H. Hoeflich.
Description: Clark, New Jersey : Talbot Publishing, an imprint of the
  Lawbook Exchange, Ltd., 2020. | Includes bibliographical references.
Identifiers: LCCN 2020045994 | ISBN 9781616196479 (hardcover)
Subjects: LCSH: Law and literature--History--19th century. | Law and
  literature--History--20th century. | Holmes, Oliver Wendell, 1809-1894.
  | Holmes, Oliver Wendell, Jr., 1841-1935. | United States. Supreme
  Court--Officials and employees. | Holmes, Sherlock--Fiction. | Private
  investigators--England--Fiction. | Doyle, Arthur Conan, 1859-1930.
  Adventure of the blue carbuncle. | Detective and mystery stories,
  English.
Classification: LCC K487.L7 H65 2020 | DDC 347.73/2634--dc23
LC record available at https://lccn.loc.gov/2020045994

Printed in the United States of America on acid-free paper

CONTENTS

Introductions   9
    M.H. Hoeflich & Ross E. Davies

Justice Holmes Reads and Reads and Reads . . .   17
    M.H. Hoeflich

The Holmeses at the Supreme Court   27
    Ross E. Davies

From Cannons to Canon: A Journey From   43
Ball's Bluff to Baker Street
    Robert S. Katz

The Adventure of the Blue Carbuncle   51
    Arthur Conan Doyle

Contributors and Credits   84

To the memory of the greatest Sherlockian
I have ever known: Professor Richard Luman;
And to the memory of the greatest legal mind
I ever encountered: Jan Deutsch;
To these two men, my teachers,
my mentors, and my friends
D.M.

M.H. Hoeflich

For Rachel S. Davies,
who taught me about Holmes
and still teaches me about justice

Ross E. Davies

In memory of the greatest Sherlockian
I have ever known:
Professor Richard Luman

Robert S. Katz

INTRODUCTIONS

One tends not to associate either Sherlock Holmes or Justice Oliver Wendell Holmes with Christmas, but, for me, it is the perfect combination. Christmas plays a small part in the Holmesian "canon" (Sherlock Holmes, that is) other than the role of a lost Christmas goose in *The Adventure of the Blue Carbuncle*. As for O.W. Holmes, one tends to think of him either sitting on the Court during its terms or relaxing in the cool New England breezes at Beverly Farms when the Court did not sit. Certainly, one could argue that neither the fictional consulting detective nor the very real Supreme Court Justice seemed overly inclined to the sort of sentimentality we associate with Christmas. Of course, we can easily imagine Holmes and Watson sitting down to their Christmas dinners only blocks away from Ebenezer Scrooge's lonely holiday repasts since both were quintessential Victorian figures . . . as was Justice Holmes. And, yet, Christmastime is one we associate with Santa and elves and reindeer rather than detectives and justices. Why then does the juxtaposition of these two figures, Holmes and Holmes, bring Christmas to my mind? The answer, as it so often does, lies with two great teachers, men who shaped my life in innumerable ways.

Richard Luman arrived at Haverford College at the same time as I did: October 1969. He came as a new Associate

Professor of Religion and I arrived as a lowly freshman. That year, each freshman was obliged to enroll in a freshman seminar. All of the faculty offering such seminars gathered together, each at a table piled with books and papers there to await inquisitive freshmen and to try to convince them to enroll in what each believed would be the most exciting seminar of them all. Richard, on the other hand, simply sat at his table reading what looked like an interesting book. I walked over and asked him what he was reading. He replied that he was engrossed in an Icelandic Saga, the *Story of Burnt Njal*. Intrigued, I asked him if he would read a few paragraphs out loud. He obliged. I then asked to see the book and was amazed to discover that he was reading the text in the original Icelandic and simultaneously translating it into perfect English for me. I was sold and signed up for his seminar on the medieval church. For an entering freshman who was Jewish, planned on majoring in Physics, and had never been in a church, this was quite an interesting choice. It was also one of the best decisions I have ever made. Richard became my friend, my mentor, my guide into the intellectual world. Richard had many passions: Icelandic history, church history, and Sherlock Holmes. Richard lent me a copy of the stories, but, of course, I did not have enough time as a first semester freshman to read all of them during the term. So, when Haverford began its Christmas break, I went home to New York and spent the entire vacation reading through the "canon." And I was hooked. Indeed, I have devoted all of Christmas vacations since then, a half-century of Christmas vacations, to reading and rereading the Sherlock Holmes stories.

If Richard Luman created the connection between Sherlock Holmes and Christmas for me, it was another teacher, Jan Deutsch, a professor at the Yale Law School, who made the connection between Justice Holmes and Christmas for me. Jan was one of those semi-mythical creatures one can only hope to encounter in one's life — a Polish refugee who completed his B.A. at Yale at 16, went to Cambridge and received a "starred first," and returned to Yale to complete both a doctorate in political science and a law degree in record time. After a brief period in practice, he returned to Yale and spent his life there. Jan, like Richard Luman, was brilliant and erudite and passionate about the life of the mind. Early in my first semester at Yale he accosted me in the hallway one morning and said that a mutual friend from Cambridge, Geoffrey Elton, had written to him and told Jan that he should get to know me since I was as eccentric as Jan was and that should make us quite compatible. And so it did. Jan fed me books (as well as regular lunches for which I, a poor law student, was exceptionally grateful). I knew very little about American law when I arrived at Yale and Jan set about remedying that gap. As the Christmas season approached, he convinced me that after exams, I should start reading the Holmes-Pollock letters because they were, in his opinion, the best way to understand the full history and scope of the ties between legal England and legal America. And so, when I would finish my apportioned lot of Sherlock Holmes during that vacation, I then turned to Justice Holmes and Sir Frederick Pollock. This combination has been my occupation and solace during every Christmas vacation since Christmas 1976. And, hence, the connection between Justice Holmes and Christmas in my life and the reason for the dedication of my contribution in this volume to these two wonderful teachers, mentors, and scholars.

— M.H. *Hoeflich*

As Professor Hoeflich nicely notes, Christmas is not prominent in the adventures of Sherlock Holmes or in the life of Oliver Wendell Holmes, and yet there can be good reasons to make the association anyway. Transitions to a New Year, in contrast, do show up in Sherlock's adventures, both explicitly and implicitly,[1] as they do from time to time in the life of Justice Holmes.[2] In that context — the annual moment that prompts reflections on the past (and sometimes even resolutions for the future) — associations are almost too easy.

A book about connections between detective Holmes and Justice Holmes offers a near-infinitude of topics on which to reflect. Given that opportunity, it seems only fair to spend a

---

1 *See, e.g.,* "The Five Orange Pips" (1891); "The Adventure of the Bruce-Partington Plans" (1908); *The Valley of Fear* (1914).

2 *See, e.g.,* Letter from Oliver Wendell Holmes, Jr. to William James (Dec. 15, 1867) (quoted in Anne C. Dailey, *Holmes and the Romantic Mind*, 48 Duke L.J. 429, 466-67 (1998)); *Fair Sex Adorns the Blue Room*, Washington Herald, Jan. 2, 1912, at 3 (New Year reception at the White House).

few pages with the essential third person: Arthur Conan Doyle, the creator of the detective. Conveniently, Conan Doyle and Justice Holmes did have a few things in common.

Consider, for example, the roles that each played as an early contributor to a form of literature that took root in their own day and has grown wildly ever since.

Conan Doyle was one of the most influential authors of detective fiction in the Western world.[3] Preceded by a few fine writers such as Edgar Allan Poe, Émile Gaboriau, Wilkie Collins, and Anna Katharine Green, he introduced Sherlock Holmes in *A Study in Scarlet* (1887) and *The Sign of Four* (1890). He then surpassed those novels by combining his important new sleuth with what may have been an equally important new form — the short-story serial featuring a recurring lead character — in *The Adventures of Sherlock Holmes*, which appeared monthly in *The Strand Magazine* from July 1891 to June 1892. To the joy of some literati and the perplexed distress of others, reading hasn't been the same since.[4] Conan

---

3 Characters such as Judge Dee — the crime-solving Chinese judge with literary roots dating back as few as 300 and as many as 1,400 years, depending on what counts and who counts — are beyond the scope of this little book.

4 *Compare, e.g.,* T.S. Eliot, *Sherlock Holmes and his Times,* 8 The Criterion 552 (Apr. 1929) (reprinted in 3 *The Complete Prose of T.S. Eliot* 601 (2015) (Frances Dickey et al., eds.)), *with* Edmund Wilson, *Why Do People Read Detective Stories?,* The New Yorker, Oct. 7, 1944.

Doyle and his creation lived[5] to witness their genre enter its "Golden Age" in the 1920s and '30s (with the rise of Agatha Christie and her near-peers) and begin its limitless branching into new forms (including, for example, early hard-boiled detectives from Dashiell Hammett and his ilk). Decades passed. Critics' forecasts that Conan Doyle and his successors would run out of stories, or that audiences would tire of them, proved consistently wrong. Tales of detection won (and still win) Pulitzer Prizes and National Book Awards. Nowadays, teachers use the original Sherlock stories as models of good writing and storytelling. "Mystery, Thriller & Suspense" is a top-level category at Amazon.com, and tales of Sherlock sell like hotcakes.

Justice Holmes was not as important to the development of law journals as Conan Doyle was to detective fiction. But he was significant, lending his good work and good name to a worthy new enterprise that would transform the legal academy. He began contributing to what is now the greatest American law journal, the *Harvard Law Review* (founded in 1887), when it was just an experiment led by a few enterprising law students. His essays on the law of agency appeared in the fledgling journal's fourth and fifth volumes in 1891, and his most celebrated article, "The Path of the Law," was published in volume ten in 1897.[6] Since then, the *Harvard Law Review*

---

5 His last Sherlock story — "The Adventure of Shoscombe Old Place" — was published in 1927, and he died in 1930.

6 O.W. Holmes, Jr., *Agency*, 4 Harv. L. Rev. 345 & 5 Harv. L. Rev. 1

method — with its distinctive mode of scholarly production, in which students select and refine works submitted by professors and other scholars — has spread nationwide. Today, every one of the 200 or so U.S. law schools publishes a whole portfolio of law reviews (at last count, Harvard itself fields 16), and tenure for a legal academic is nearly impossible without a c.v. that includes works published in law reviews.

There are other parallels and connections between Conan Doyle and Justice Holmes. Weightily, they were, in a sense, mirror images of each other. The former was a great writer about crime who did more than merely dabble in the administration of justice. The latter was a great justice who did more than merely dabble in legal literature.[7] Amusingly, both read Ronald Knox.[8] And intriguingly, there are more. But those inquiries must await another day.

— *Ross E. Davies*

(1891); O.W. Holmes, *The Path of the Law*, 10 Harv. L. Rev. 457 (1897).

7 *See, e.g.*, Arthur Conan Doyle, *The Case of Oscar Slater* (1912); O.W. Holmes, Jr., *The Common Law* (1881).

8 *See, e.g.*, Arthur Conan Doyle to Ronald Knox, July 5, 1912, *reprinted in* Nicholas Utechin, *From Piff-Pouff to Backnecke*, Baker Street Journal 44-45 (Christmas 2010); M.H. Hoeflich et al., *The Black Book* (2020) (1934 entry for "Ronald A. Knox — Settled Out of Court").

Justice Oliver Wendell Holmes, of the
Massachusettes Supreme Judicial Court (circa 1890).

16

JUSTICE HOLMES READS AND READS AND READS . . .

<><><><><><><><><><><><><><><><><><><><><>

M.H. HOEFLICH

Justice Holmes was larger than life, in the oft-repeated words of one of his many admiring biographers; he was an Olympian.[1] He was tall, aristocratic, his face adorned with a magnificent handlebar mustache, the descendant of generations of lawyers, scholars, and professors. His capacity for work was enormous. His commitment to excellence and personal success was unrivaled. He survived crippling wounds and hellish imprisonment that killed lesser men and he lived far beyond the biblically allotted three score years and ten. And he was remote, like a true Olympian. He stayed above the political fray and the controversies that plagued lesser men in an age of controversy and conflict.[2] But he was also a man with an enormous capacity for reading and entertainment. When work was done, he loved distraction. And the distraction

---

1 Catherine Drinker Bowen, *Justice from Olympus* (1944).

2 But see, Brad Snyder, "The House that Built Holmes," *Law & Hist. Rev.*, Aug. 2012, v. 30, n. 3, pp. 661-720.

that he loved most was reading. Walton Hale Hamilton, an economist and member of the Yale Law School faculty, in a now little-cited and underrated, but wonderful, essay on the Holmes-Pollock correspondence, wrote:

> Holmes read — or at least exposed himself — to everything, and the range is as staggering as the sheer bulk. His inhibitions were few. "A picture of a squalid and worthless life is a kind of art in which I take little pleasure." He avoided the Civil War, passed up biography, shied at mathematics and government reports, regarded polysyllabic erudition as not for him. For general information he went to the encyclopedias, the volumes of *Everyman's Library*, the books of the *Home University* which generally gave a fillip or a fact. He roamed through the classics, literature and philosophy, the current social scene, the exploration of strange lands, the nature of the physical universe. He delighted in Fabre's insects told about in "truly golden books"; was carried away by Nansen's *Farthest North*; got only "a very blurry impression" of Whitehead's *Science and the Modern World* — but hoped he had the general drift. He found great cisterns of delight in Reinach's *Cults* and drew his ration of gloom from the *New Republic*. But as his eye moved down the page, interest had to go along; and the idea that he read to elevate he met with scorn. His "Thank God, I am a man of low taste" applies in the library as well as at burlesque. He always kept Balzac at hand and on occasion "alleviated my serious reading in Rabelais with McKechnie's *Magna Carta*." He did not mind a book which would call a blush to "the cheek of my innocence" and rather delighted in one which described "unspeakable practices on the part of the heroine." He loved to have on his shelves books hot from the press and

books that were old before America was discovered; books that show the same human feelings we have today and books that lead into the great unknown. It is as absurd to be afraid of any book as it is to be afraid of any case.[3]

The voracity with which Holmes read books (and some articles) is evidenced, above all, in the notebook he kept by his side for more than a half century, the so-called *Black Book*.[4] This volume contains lists of his reading from 1881 until 1935. During these years he read dozens of books each year. Many were quite serious works on law, philosophy, history, and art in English, French, and German (with the occasional classical text thrown in for good measure). Others were what are called "light reading," ranging from children's books to romantic novels to adventure tales and many, many detective novels. Justice Holmes was a devotee, perhaps it would not be an exaggeration to say an "obsessive" devotee, of the detective novel. These he would read — or have read to him — out loud in the evenings, often in the summers away from Washington and the Court, as he and Fanny rested in the cool of an evening at their beloved "Beverly Farms."

---

3 Walton Hale Hamilton, "On Dating Mr. Justice Holmes," *The University of Chicago Law Review*, v. 9, (1941), 1-29, at 12-13.

4 A tentative transcription with introductory essays is now published: M.H. Hoeflich et al., *The Black Book* (2020). There exist two other shorter notebooks in which Holmes kept lists of his reading as a young man; see, E.N. Little, "The early reading of Justice Oliver Wendell Holmes," *Harvard Library Bulletin*, v. 8 (1954), at 163-203.

In spite of the fact that Justice Holmes devoured hundreds of detective novels during the half century in which he kept a record of his reading in the *Black Book*, there is little mention of this pastime in his voluminous correspondence with friends and colleagues. Indeed, the two printed volumes of Holmes' longest and most personal correspondence with Sir Frederick Pollock, the great English jurist and Holmes' personal friend, contain only a few brief references to detective fiction. In his correspondence with Pollock, Holmes makes brief mention of Wilkie Collins, Émile Gaboriau, Katharine Green, and, of course, Conan Doyle's Sherlock Holmes. This is particularly surprising both because Holmes read so much in the genre and because so much of the correspondence with Pollock is taken up by discussions of books the two men had read. In fact, Holmes speaks quite frequently of other genres of "light fiction," often in the same letter as a discussion of a weightier tome. In a letter to Pollock on 26 August 1926, for instance, Holmes wrote:

> . . . the book that has made me laugh, and which I don't send only because it would be too local to hit you is *Nize Baby*, the goings on and talk on the different floors of a New York apartment house. A book I am reading with pleasure Höffding, *History of Modern Philosophy*.[5]

The juxtaposition of a comedy of manners with a volume of Germanic philosophical history is one that, if not unique to

---

5   M.A. De Wolfe Howe, *Holmes-Pollock Letters*, II.188.

Holmes, is certainly unusual. But, in fact, the idea that Holmes could read and enjoy a comic exposition of the social life of New Yorkers and a weighty tome on German philosophy is illustrative of Holmes' approach to reading. Holmes' reading may be put into three categories: (1) reading for work, *i.e.* law, government, and economics; (2) reading for self-improvement; and (3) reading for distraction and pure entertainment. Holmes took his law-related reading seriously and he pursued it with a vengeance. One need only read through his comments on the books he read in preparation for writing the essays that became *The Common Law* to recognize that Holmes was the paradigmatic "pragmatic reader."[6] His notes on these books are detailed, multi-lingual, and often contain multiple cross-references to other sources. But, as I stated earlier, Holmes believed that when work was finished, he was free to pursue other activities. Nevertheless, Holmes was very much a man of the nineteenth century and even free time was supposed to be devoted — at least in part — to uplifting efforts at self-improvement. Thus, when Holmes read volumes of history, philosophy, politics, art, and other culturally enriching subjects he was reading for pleasure and not for work, but pleasure that was also uplifting and educational. Unlike some of his contemporaries who eschewed frivolous reading of novels, however, Holmes also enjoyed reading comedies, adventure tales, romantic novels, and detective stories. These

---

6 *See* M.H. Hoeflich, "The Lawyer as Pragmatic Reader," *University of Arkansas Law Review.*

were, for a good Victorian, books with no purpose other than pure entertainment, but for the hard-working Justice Holmes these were precisely the type of books that he could enjoy on a summer's evening with his beloved wife, Fanny. They provided an escape from the harsh realities of the world Holmes knew so well and with which he had to deal in his judicial life.

Justice Holmes' comments in his letters to Frederick Pollock bear out this categorization. On 24 February 1923, Holmes wrote to Pollock:

> . . . I have been listening in the evening to two or three thrillers, the last, *Bull Dog Drummond*. Wilkie Collins was right that what men want is a story.[7]

On 10 February 1925, Holmes wrote:

> . . . We are reading for the first time some of A.K. Green's detective stories . . . she excels in making false clues, but the supposed real facts and the ultimate explanations are rather too elaborate to be credible. The manner (apt to be tedious in narrative) is much like Wilkie Collins; it may be only the general fashion of the time.[8]

On 17 February 1932, Holmes finally spoke of Sherlock Holmes:

> I am going through the Sherlock Holmes stories with a good deal of pleasure. He is better than his imitators. I am about

---

7 *Holmes-Pollock Letters*, II.114.

8 *Ibid.*, II.154.

to turn to graver matters. A little book by Wm. McDougall, *World Chaos* . . . to be followed by a big dull one not yet seen and title forgotten. . . . It is time that I turn to other interests than murder.[9]

And on 17 March 1932, Holmes wrote:

> I have finished C.D. Broad's *The Mind & Its Place in Nature*. That is, it was read in my presence — I taking an occasional snooze — not thinking much of the work & finding it very dull as well as not believing it. I have sweetened it by rereading all Sherlock Holmes & *The Moonstone* which I think the best there is in that line.[10]

And here, in a few brief paragraphs, is the key to Holmes reading Holmes. He loved detective fiction, although he read with a critical eye (and, not surprisingly found Conan Doyle and Wilkie Collins to be the best of the genre's authors). But for Holmes, detective fiction was a secret passion, what he called an "ignoble liking."[11] He explained, in another letter to Pollock, that he rarely read biographies. Why? Because he did not have the time "and other subjects interest me more."[12] As Walton Hale Hamilton divined, it was terribly important for Mr. Justice Holmes to be seen as a serious sort:

---

9   *Ibid.*, II.304.

10 *Ibid.*, II.305.

11 *Ibid.*, II.294.

12 *Ibid.*, II.269. And see, also, II.126: "I don't read biographies, as a rule, or Life & Letters, or books about the war. I have to confine myself to my subjects, with excursions into literature, as last summer, for levity."

His father had not permitted him to leave his lessons undone; and as a man he was too conscientious to neglect his cases. He rather liked to think of himself as taking his tasks more seriously than the evidence seems to warrant. He is constantly under "a high pressure of work" or subject to "much strenuous toil." He has only a minute and a half to write to Pollock before doing something else but it is ever thus. The *Common Law* has cost him hundreds of hours of sleep which he never expects to recover — though he did try to get a little installment back now and then, before his brethren or other friends came to dinner. Forever he envied the leisure which other men seemed to possess.[13]

Justice Holmes was not only one of the greatest jurists to sit on the United States Supreme Court, the author of one of the greatest synthetic legal works, *The Common Law*, an heir of Boston's intellectual "gods," but, also, not surprisingly a man of many sides and many emotions. In the *Black Book* he noted the plants and flowers as they came up each Spring in Washington, equally took delight in criticizing esoteric points in German legal scholarship, and noted every book he read for half a century, including those that reflected his "ignoble liking": detective fiction.

It would, perhaps, be too much to say that Justice Holmes and Sherlock Holmes shared certain characteristics: a disdain for mankind but a soft heart for the foibles of men and women, a critical intelligence that could dissect the most complex problems and reduce them to pithy maxims, a searching

---

13 Hamilton, art. cit., above, n. 3, at 7.

intelligence constantly in need of stimulation, and a need for distraction. In the case of Justice Holmes it was fiction, including detective stories. In the case of Sherlock Holmes, it was playing the violin badly. But, then, again, perhaps it would not be too much to see these similarities between the real jurist and the fictional consulting detective. Not at all.

*Justice Oliver Wendell Holmes, of the Supreme Court
of the United States, greets the Press (March 8, 1926).*

THE HOLMESES AT THE SUPREME COURT

◇◇◇◇◇◇◇◇◇◇◇◇◇◇◇◇◇◇◇◇◇◇◇◇◇◇◇◇

ROSS E. DAVIES

The great Justice Oliver Wendell Holmes brought the great detective Sherlock Holmes to the U.S. Supreme Court. (To keep things simple, I will call the Justice "Holmes" and the detective "Sherlock.") Before Holmes joined the Supreme Court in 1902, neither Sherlock nor his creator, Arthur Conan Doyle, had ever appeared in any opinions issued by the Court, or in any pleadings filed there. Nor had the newspapers shown much interest in connecting Sherlock to the Court in print. But after the arrival of Holmes, the associations picked up quickly, and persisted. I know of no evidence that Holmes intended any of these entanglements with Sherlock (save one, as we will see in a moment), but an objective observer (he prided himself on his objectivity) would not have been surprised. There were, after all, so many notable parallels — the name, the dispassionate yet adventurous genius, the long and angular physique, the seeming indestructability, the ever-increasing renown.

27

Holmes took his seat on the Supreme Court bench for the first time on December 8, 1902.[1] Within a few weeks, the newspapers were tethering him to Sherlock in the public eye. The *New York Times*, for example, published this anecdote on January 18, 1903:

> According to a distinguished after-dinner speaker who was telling stories at a dinner at Sherry's, a certain Westerner who figures very largely in Wall Street read in the newspapers about the appointment of Justice Holmes to a vacancy on the bench of the United States Supreme Court.
>
> "Who is this Judge Holmes?" inquired the Westerner of an acquaintance. "Is he a son of Sherlock Holmes?"
>
> "No," said the acquaintance. "Don't you know that Sherlock Holmes is not a real character?"
>
> The Westerner was surprised, and his companion added:
>
> "Judge Holmes is a son of Oliver Wendell Holmes." [Holmes père — a nineteenth-century polymath and author of, among many works, the popular "Breakfast Table" essays in *The Atlantic Monthly* — was more famous than his judicial son at this time.]
>
> "Who in thunder is he? I never heard of him before," said the Westerner.[2]

---

1   Journal of the Supreme Court of the United States 56 (Dec. 8, 1902).

2   N.Y. Times Magazine Supplement, Jan. 18, 1903, at 2. This is a neat example of coastal mockery of flyover country bumpkins even before the advent of overflights, and — with the appearance of the anecdote in newspapers serving the middle of the country — also an example of the capacity of the bumpkins to enjoy a joke at their own expense. *See, e.g.,* Mansfield [Ohio] News, Jan. 30, 1903, at 4; Oberlin [Kansas] Times,

Holmes served on the Supreme Court for nearly 30 years,[3] and little stories along similar lines continued to appear from time to time throughout his long career. In 1909, for example, the *National Tribune* (of Washington, DC) published this one:

> Sometimes, you know, you just think it is no use at all. During inaugural times some of the visitors to Washington really seemed to have holes in their heads where the bump of knowledge ought to be. For instance, one lady was showing some men about the city — men of some means, fair education and good business understanding. "That man is Mr. Justice Holmes," said the lady, pointing out the famous son of a famous father, who is now on the Supreme Bench and who has also a gallant record and four wounds as a Colonel in the Union army.
>
> "Holmes — Holm — oh, yes! Now, really, you don't say so? Is that sure enough Sherlock Holmes? Well, I declare! He doesn't look a bit as I expected him to. Say, but isn't he just great? I've read every one of his books." And the lady let it go at that.[4]

I do not know what Holmes thought of all this. But knowing (as we do, from Professor Hoeflich's essay in this volume) that

---

Apr. 17, 1903, at 6. Indeed, a version of this story, without the mockery, had circulated in the Midwest in the summer of 1902, around the time President Theodore Roosevelt first nominated Holmes to the Court. *See Not an Ohio Man*, Richmond Dispatch, Aug. 20, 1902, at 4 (quoting the *Cleveland Plain Dealer*).

3 His last day on the bench was January 11, 1932. Journal of the Supreme Court of the United States 161 (Jan. 11, 1932), 168 (Jan. 12, 1932), 169-70 (Jan. 13, 1932).

4 National Tribune, Mar. 25, 1909, at 5.

he liked the stories of Sherlock's adventures, surely we can safely assume he was pleased, or perhaps merely amused, but certainly not annoyed.

Then there is the serious business of the Supreme Court — cases. Coincidentally (surely), the first Sherlockian pleading in the Court's history arrived shortly after Holmes did.

In 1901, the U.S. Postmaster General had issued regulations under which publications "having the characteristics of books" would no longer qualify as "periodicals" mailable at the relatively low second-class rates intended for newspapers and the like, but would instead go at the higher third-class rates.[5] Several publishers challenged the change in court. They won their cases (there were three of them — *Houghton v. Payne, Smith v. Payne,* and *Bates & Guild Co. v. Payne*) at the trial court level. But the Postmaster General appealed and the appellate court reversed the trial court's decisions.

So, the publishers appealed to the Supreme Court. The transcript of record in *Smith v. Payne* was filed in the Court on November 14, 1903 — less than one year after Holmes joined the Court. It included this passage from one of the pleadings in the case:

---

5 Annual Reports of the Post-Office Departments for the Fiscal Year Ended June 30, 1901, at 772-83 (1901); *Payne v. National Railway Publishing Co.,* 20 App. D.C. 581, 585-86 (D.C. Cir. 1902). For a great mass of detail about this episode, see Ross E. Davies, *The Regulatory Adventure of the Two Norwood Builders,* 2015 Green Bag Almanac 567.

> Each issue contains high-class fiction of great literary merit, such as "The Sherlock Holmes Detective Stories," by A. Conan Doyle, "An Accidental Password," by Nicholas Carter, and "The Clique of Gold," by Emile Gaboriau . . . .[6]

To no avail. The publishers lost. The Court's decisions in all three cases were by identical 7-2 votes, with Justice Henry Billings Brown writing for the majority (joined by Justices David J. Brewer, Edward Douglass White, Rufus W. Peckham, Joseph McKenna, Oliver Wendell Holmes, and William R. Day), and Justice John Marshall Harlan dissenting (joined by Chief Justice Melville W. Fuller).[7]

In his opinions for the Court, Brown did not mention Sherlock by name, but in his *Smith v. Payne* opinion Brown did make an unkind comment in passing:

> The books of these series are apparently of an inferior class of literature . . . .[8]

Despite his appreciation for "'The Sherlock Holmes Detective Stories,' by A. Conan Doyle" (see again Professor Hoeflich's essay), Holmes joined Brown's opinion. I take Holmes's silence on this matter to mean that he viewed the aspersion cast on the Sherlock stories as a dictum too slight (and maybe also too obviously wrong) to merit picking a fight in the pages of the

---

6 Transcript of Record 2 (filed Nov. 14, 1903), *Smith v. Payne*, 194 U.S. 104 (1904).

7 194 U.S. 88 (1904); 194 U.S. 104 (1904); 194 U.S. 106 (1904).

8 *Smith v. Payne*, 194 U.S. at 105.

United States Reports. Conan Doyle himself, however, might have concurred with Brown. He viewed his Sherlock stories (which he called "police romances") as "on a different and humbler plane" than "my more serious literary work."[9]

Sherlock continued to appear occasionally in pleadings during Holmes's tenure, though he was not referred to by name in a reported Supreme Court opinion.[10] After Holmes's retirement, there was a three-year hiatus in citations to Sherlock,[11] after which they returned and then continued into the twenty-first century — including, in recent years, mentions by name in reported opinions.[12]

Eventually, Holmes was joined on the Supreme Court by other great figures in the law with connections to Sherlock. The two most prominent members of this elite within an elite were Charles Evans Hughes and Louis D. Brandeis.

---

9 A. Conan Doyle, *Preface to the Author's Edition, The White Company* vi (1891; 1902 D. Appleton edition); Arthur Conan Doyle, *Preface, The Case-Book of Sherlock Holmes* xix, xx (1927; 2007 Gasogene Books edition, Leslie S. Klinger, editor).

10 *See, e.g.,* Transcript of Record 250-51 (filed Apr. 11, 1910), *Smith v. Hitchcock,* 226 U.S. 53 (1912); Transcript of Record 237 (filed Sept. 27, 1920), *Schurmann v. U.S.,* 257 U.S. 621 (1922).

11 *Compare* note 3 above (Holmes retired on January 11, 1932, *with* Petitioner's Brief, Appendix at 28 (filed Jan. 14, 1935), *Fox Film Corporation v. Muller,* 294 U.S. 696 (1935).

12 *See, e.g., I.N.S. v. St. Cyr,* 533 U.S. 289, 320 n.44 (2001).

Chief Justice Charles Evans Hughes (left) and
senior Associate Justice Oliver Wendell Holmes (1931).

When Hughes took his seat on the Court in 1910, he was already known as a Sherlock enthusiast. At least as far back as 1907 (when he was governor of New York), newspapers had reported that "Conan Doyle is one of his favorite authors; Sherlock Holmes one of his favorite characters."[13] After a few years on the bench, Hughes resigned in 1916 to contest with Woodrow Wilson for the presidency of the United States. Hughes would return to the Supreme Court in 1930 to serve as Chief Justice. In the years between his stints on

13 *Charles Evans Hughes, the Man*, New-York Daily Tribune, June 23, 1907, at 3.

the Court, his engagement in public service continued, as did
his connections to Sherlock. In 1918, for example, President
Wilson enlisted Hughes to assist the U.S. Department of
Justice in an investigation of corruption in the production of
military aircraft.[14] In its July 11 issue, *Life* magazine made light
of the investigation in what was (and perhaps remains) the
only portrayal of a current or former Justice as Sherlock in a
political cartoon:

Sherlock Holmes: WE ARE NOW ON THE TRACK OF A DANGEROUS GERMAN.
Department of Justice: MARVELOUS! MARVELOUS, HOLMES! I DON'T SEE
HOW YOU DISCOVER THOSE THINGS.

The cartoon was accompanied by a sarcastic comparison of
Hughes to Sherlock:

> Only yesterday there was an airplane investigation on,
> a scandal that made strong men turn pale and even some
> Democrats shudder. Nearly a billion dollars had been
> spent, and nothing to show for it. And then Mr. Charles
> Evans Hughes, in comparison with whom Old Sleuth in

---

14 Albert W. Fox, *Hughes Is Made Aide in Aircraft Inquiry*, Washington
Post, May 16, 1918, at 1.

his palmiest days looked like a Kansas rube in a Saratoga gambling hell — Mr. Hughes was appointed to throw the limelight on this horrible scandal, that all men might know what had happened and where the money had gone. But oblivion was waiting with distended jaw. It was a fairly full meal, but oblivion gobbled it down. He now holds Mr. Hughes and the airplane scandal in his capacious maw.[15]

Brandeis followed Holmes and Hughes onto the Supreme Court in 1916. Of the three, Brandeis came to the Court with the strongest public record of Sherlockian connections. Those connections were on full display in the newspaper coverage of his work on Congressional hearings into the biggest Washington political scandal of 1910, and perhaps the most consequential scandal before Watergate: the "Pinchot-Ballinger affair." In short, U.S. Forest Service Chief Gifford Pinchot and some environmental conservationists working with him and in the U.S. Department of the Interior accused newly appointed (by President William Howard Taft) Secretary of the Interior Richard Ballinger of shady dealings involving coal field leases in Alaska. Taft, Ballinger, and Attorney General George Wickersham closed ranks to defend Ballinger. Meetings were held, documents were generated, Ballinger kept his job, his critics were dealt with, leaks ensued, and congressional hearings followed.

Brandeis represented the Ballinger critics at the hearings, where his characteristically thorough research, inexorable

---

15 *Lest We Remember*, Life, July 11, 1918, at 100.

reasoning, and incisive questioning exposed all: Ballinger may not have been criminally corrupt in his dealings with the coal-mining interests, but he was a mean-spirited, machine-style partisan who had lied about details of his collaboration with Taft and Wickersham against critics in his own department and the Forest Service. There was one document in particular that Brandeis struggled to discover and the Taft Administration strove to conceal from him. When the "smoking gun" document (it wasn't called that at the time, but the modern label fits) finally came to light, it showed that Ballinger wasn't the only liar: Taft and Wickersham had lied too. The lying and the underlying treatment of environmentalist staff inflamed already strained relations between Taft and his predecessor, Theodore Roosevelt, which in turn fostered a split in the Republican Party that enabled Democrat Woodrow Wilson to win the 1912 presidential election.[16] It would be 60 years before another presidential cover-up would so clearly cost a political party a chance to occupy the White House.

In 1910, though, the powerful pols had managed to hold onto their jobs for the time being. The newspapers had a field day nevertheless, and Brandeis was the hero of the hour. Stories about the Pinchot-Ballinger affair — with headlines like "Uses Methods of Great Sherlock Holmes" and "Louis Brandeis, People's Detective, Solves Mysteries a la Sherlock Holmes" — splashed across the continent. Versions of the leading story,

---

16 The best compact treatment of Brandeis's role in this business is Melvin I. Urosfky, *Louis D. Brandeis: A Life* ch. 11 (2009).

which appeared in several papers, covered not only Brandeis's work on the case, but also his thinking on the subject of Sherlock, which was three-fold.

First, Brandeis was an established appreciator not only of the Sherlock stories, but also of detective fiction generally:

> Brandeis reads detective stories for a diversion. He likes Sherlock Holmes best of all.[17]

Second, Brandeis was conscious of similarities between his own approach to cases and Sherlock's:

> "I use practically the same method," he said to me. "It's a matter of having special knowledge and being able to draw the only possible conclusion."[18]

And third, Brandeis liked the idea of engaging in a wider range of Sherlockian investigations:

> "I have never tried to solve actual police mysteries. Yes, I think I should like to try to catch a murderer some time."[19]

Some other Justices who served on the Supreme Court during Holmes's years there also had connections to Sherlock. Owen J. Roberts, for example, who served from 1930 to 1945, was compared in print to the detective both before

---

17 Robert F. Wilson, *Louis Brandeis, People's Detective, Solves Mysteries a la Sherlock Holmes*, Wiles-Barre Times-Leader, June 9, 1910, at 3.

18 *Id.*; *Uses Methods of Great Sherlock Holmes*, Vancouver (B.C.) Daily Province, June 17, 1910, at 9 ("He laughingly says that his system of deduction is practically that of Sherlock Holmes.").

19 *Louis Brandeis, People's Detective, Solves Mysteries Like a Real She[r]lock*

and during his time on the Court.[20] But there were also Justices who seemingly were unaware of the great detective — William R. Day, for example, who served from 1903 to 1922.[21] And there are many more Justices about whom a definite claim cannot yet be made. So, a complete roster of those who served with Holmes and related somehow to Sherlock must await further research.

Brandeis made his appreciation of Sherlock public. Holmes did not. We know he liked the stories, but what did he think of the character? Did Holmes himself feel any connection to Sherlock himself? The answer, pleasingly, is yes. He said so, late in life.

On March 8, 1930, just a few days after Hughes returned to the Supreme Court as Chief Justice, both Justice Edward T. Sanford and retired Chief Justice William Howard Taft

---

Holmes, Tacoma Times, June 23, 1910, at 3.

20 *See, e.g.*, Lemuel F. Parton, *Supreme Court Justice Said Most Impartial Man*, Dayton Daily News, Mar. 6, 1934, at 13 ("[I]t was as a Sherlock Holmes that Mr. Roberts made his case."); Raymond Clapper, *Government Counsel Flays Patriotic Defense As Bunk; Denounces Fall and Doheny*, San Bernardino Daily Sun, Dec. 14, 1926, at 2.

21 *See, e.g.*, *Stories Told of Judge and Jury*, Omaha Sunday Bee, July 21, 1901, pt. 2, at 7 ("It was not very long ago that he blandly inquired of a barrister fond of literary allusions, 'And who is Sherlock Holmes?' following up the clue when it was given him with that quiet persistence which is the glory of the bench, 'Yes, and who is Conan Doyle?'").

died. As Chief Justice, Hughes was by duty bound to attend the funerals. During Hughes's absence, the senior Justice — Holmes — served as acting Chief Justice. One of Holmes's tasks was to send official notice of the sad news to the U.S. Senate. In his biography of Brandeis, Lewis J. Paper provides a cinematic scene of the acting Chief at work, and channeling Sherlock:

> . . . Holmes enjoyed being the temporary chief justice — it injected a little variety into his life. So he was quite happy to give the senators the document they wanted. He took out his pen and then turned to [Reynolds Robinson, the Chief Justice's law clerk]. To whom do I address this letter? The president of the Senate, the clerk responded. Holmes began to write, and then stopped. Who's the president of the Senate, he asked Robertson. The vice president of the United States, came the reply. Holmes began to write and then stopped again. Who's the vice president now? Robertson provided the name of Charles Curtis and Holmes, now satisfied, drafted the note and then looked up at Robertson. "I'm like Sherlock Holmes," said the senior justice. "I don't keep inconsequential facts in my head."[22]

Holmes knew what he was talking about.[23] He was referring to a memorable scene in the first Sherlock story ever

---

22 Lewis J. Paper, *Brandeis* 326, 426 n.1 (1983) (citing "Interview with Francis Kirkham, April 27, 1981. Robertson related this incident to Kirkham, who succeeded Robertson as Hughes's clerk."). I thank Robert A. James, a lawyer with a Holmesian reading range, for bringing this passage to my attention.

23 At least one post-mortem profile suggested that Holmes's study of Sherlock began after his retirement from the Court. *Justice Holmes:*

published, *A Study in Scarlet*. The narrator of the story — Dr. John H. Watson — recalls a disconcerting conversation with Sherlock in which the detective explains his weirdly selective memory (which some scholars believe is really an elaborate pulling of Dr. Watson's leg):

> . . . My surprise reached a climax, however, when I found incidentally that he was ignorant of the Copernican Theory and of the composition of the Solar System. That any civilized human being in this nineteenth century should not be aware that the earth travelled round the sun appeared to be to me such an extraordinary fact that I could hardly realize it.
>
> "You appear to be astonished," he said, smiling at my expression of surprise. "Now that I do know it I shall do my best to forget it."
>
> "To forget it!"
>
> "You see," he explained, "I consider that a man's brain originally is like a little empty attic, and you have to stock it with such furniture as you choose. A fool takes in all the lumber of every sort that he comes across, so that the knowledge which might be useful to him gets crowded out, or at best is jumbled up with a lot of other things so that he has a difficulty in laying his hands upon it. Now the skilful workman is very careful indeed as to what he takes into his brain-attic. . . . Depend upon it there comes a time when for every addition of knowledge you forget something that you

---

Yankee Philosopher, Asbury Park Evening Press, Mar. 12, 1935, at 7; *see also, e.g., Mystery — And Literature*, Courier-Post (Camden, NJ), Jan. 25, 1933, at 8. But we know better now. It began in the nineteenth century. *See* M.H. Hoeflich et al., *The Black Book* (2020) (1893 entry for "Conan Doyle, Study in Scarlet &c. &c.").

knew before. It is of the highest importance, therefore, not to have useless facts elbowing out the useful ones."

"But the Solar System!" I protested.

"What the deuce is it to me?" he interrupted impatiently . . . .[24]

There we have it. Justice Oliver Wendell Holmes really was a Sherlock Holmes at the Supreme Court.

---

24 *A Study in Scarlet*, Beeton's Christmas Annual 1, 9 (1887).

Captain Oliver Wendell Holmes, of the
20th Massachusettes Regiment (circa 1862).

FROM CANNONS TO CANON
A JOURNEY FROM BALL'S BLUFF
TO BAKER STREET

◇◇◇◇◇◇◇◇◇◇◇◇◇◇◇◇◇◇◇◇◇◇◇◇◇◇◇◇◇

ROBERT S. KATZ

Two truths have by now likely become self-evident in this chapbook. First, Oliver Wendell Holmes, Jr, was an aficionado of the stories of Sherlock Holmes. Second, his participation in the American Civil War was a seminal event for OWH. On the surface, these issues seem unrelated. Yet, a more careful look at the war experiences of OWH and the stories of Sherlock Holmes might provide a linkage between these two superficially disparate events. More importantly, their association and relationship might also provide an insight into the reading habits and emotions of this great jurist.

The wartime service of OWH in the Twentieth Massachusetts Infantry has been described both well and in detail elsewhere, especially the G. Edward White biography.[1] What matters here is that OWH was wounded three times. First, in the chest/breast area (at Ball's Bluff). Then in the neck, at Antietam. Finally, he was wounded in the heel during

---

1   G. Edward White, *Justice Oliver Wendell Holmes* ch. 2 (1993).

the Chancellorsville Campaign. Surviving even a single wound in the era when medicine was more harm than help is remarkable. Living through three potentially fatal injuries is nothing short of miraculous and demonstrates something about the constitution of the man. Perhaps it's no surprise that he lived to such great old age. To make bad matters worse, OWH also suffered a severe bout of dysentery, just prior to the battle of Fredericksburg. This gastrointestinal infection, with profound diarrhea and bloody stool (then colloquially called "the bloody flux") was often more lethal than shot and shell. Again, OWH lived through that as well. Modern day writers and armchair psychiatrists might speculate that these left OWH with some form of what we now call PTSD. Ruminating on that would take us far afield from our topic and likely add little to our exploration of Oliver and Sherlock. But the Civil War did stay with Holmes the jurist and, more significantly, Holmes the reader.

Perhaps the essence of this essay can be distilled down to one simple question. Why was OWH interested in and by the stories of Sherlock Holmes? Was there anything unique to them amongst all the literary avenues open to OWH that caused him to focus his attention on what some regard as mere popular fiction?

Let's first deal with the easy part, which is that they both have the same last name!! In fact, Arthur Conan Doyle's mother was known to be fond of the works of OWH, Sr. Michael Sims, in his *Arthur and Sherlock*, believes that it was likely that Conan Doyle picked the name Holmes for this reason.[2] He does, nevertheless, admit that there were other examples of the Holmes name throughout England at the time. Mattias Bostrom, in his *From Holmes to Sherlock*, comes to a similar conclusion.[3] This theory has the benefit of plausibility and may well be correct. Yet, while it might explain why the books first caught the eye of OWH, it does not help us to understand OWH's lifelong readings of the stories and his attachment to them. Beyond the catchiness of the name, there needs to be a great deal more depth to retain this level of interest.

To understand why OWH found the stories of Sherlock Holmes, known collectively as "The Canon," we need to turn to the stories themselves.

The first of the Holmes stories, *A Study in Scarlet*, is a short novel that begins, not with Sherlock Holmes (he comes along a few pages later) but with a brief autobiographical sketch of an equally remarkable character — John H. Watson, MD. Watson tells us, in just a few short pages that give us a whirlwind introduction to an extraordinary early manhood, that after medical training, he joined the army. Sent to Afghanistan, he is seriously wounded in the shoulder (an anatomic site not far from OWH's first injury) at the Battle of Maiwand. Hauled off the battlefield, where he would have faced certain death, by his orderly,

2 Michael Sims, *Arthur and Sherlock* 23, 114 (2017).

3 Mattias Boström, *From Holmes to Sherlock* 25 (2013; Eng. trans. 2017).

he is taken to hospital. During his recovery, he contracts "enteric fever" (usually typhoid or paratyphoid) with the same abdominal pain and bloody bowel movements that OWH would have suffered.

As the stories progress, other mentions of the Civil War appear. In "The Five Orange Pips," one of the characters served under Jackson and Hood and eventually joined the KKK, an organization founded by former Confederates including Nathan Bedford Forrest.

To make matters both more complex and simultaneously more relevant, there's the matter of "Watson's wandering wound," as it's known in Sherlockian circles. Noted earlier is the explicit description of Watson's having been shot in the shoulder. In the second of the Holmes stories, *The Sign of Four*, Watson alluded to a bullet having hit in the region of his Achilles tendon, rather near the heel. There's a further mention of the wound site, or sites, which will be discussed presently. The attempt to identify what really happened to Watson has caused the largest effusion of ink, diagnosis, and speculation in the Sherlockian literature, which is itself vast. The relevant issue here is that OWH would have been well aware of Watson's battlefield trauma, the relation of the gunshot wounds to his own, and even the terrible bout with a diarrheal illness, common to nineteenth century armies.

The most important Canonical reference to the American Civil War is so critical that it appears not once but twice. Perhaps it was Conan Doyle's favorite bit of Sherlockian deduction and wizardry. At the opening of "The Cardboard

Box," Holmes essentially reads the mind of John Watson. From the movements of his head and the expressions on his face, Holmes deduces that Watson is thinking of the Civil War, war in general, and Watson's own personal encounter with violent conflict, as Watson's hand moves towards his own wound, wherever that's located. We also learn that Watson owned a portrait of Henry Ward Beecher, whose sister Harriet was acquainted with OWH, Sr.[4] Holmes speculates on the gallantry shown in the Civil War and the preposterous nature of war as a means of conflict resolution.

As the story deals with issues that were then regarded as of a somewhat sexual nature, "The Cardboard Box" did not appear in the anthology version of the collected group of stories. In spite of that, Conan Doyle must have liked this introductory segment so much that he simply lifted it and used it in a subsequent short story, "The Resident Patient." That story appeared in a different anthology collection and, some years later, "Cardboard Box" made it into a subsequent anthology. One can imagine the confusion of the first time reader in coming across the identical introductory section in two entirely separate stories. Nonetheless, it's perhaps the finest moment of Sherlockian deduction as well as an insight into the war experiences of John Watson. It also demonstrates that Sherlock Holmes himself had a considerable familiarity with America's greatest event.

---

4 *Justice Oliver Wendell Holmes* at 183.

There is no question that the American Civil War had a profound influence on the subsequent life and thoughts of OWH. He lost many friends during the conflict and came close to himself dying perhaps as many as four times. One cannot emerge from that maelstrom unchanged. But one of the perhaps more pleasant aspects of his war experience was that it brought out his interest in the Sherlock Holmes stories.

Of course, it's easy to suggest that a great legal mind and jurist would be attracted to the deductions of Holmes, the intricacies of the plots, the world around Baker Street. However, all of those may not have really been the "hook" that caught the affections of OWH. The reader must be aware that while Sherlock Holmes is the protagonist, the star, the center of attraction, he's not the narrator. What we know about Sherlock is what his biographer, John Watson, chooses to tell us. The stories are told through the words of an observer, certainly a participant, with his own life story as a major aspect of the Canon.

Oliver Wendell Holmes, Jr, was a young man who went to war. He was wounded multiple times, suffered a ghastly infection along with everything else. Yet when his service was finished, he returned home and had to begin an entirely new life and career. The war would always affect him. John Watson, as a young physician, also volunteered for the army. He was sent to a strange and foreign place where he was badly wounded, perhaps even wounded twice and in places rather similar to those of OWH. He had a similar gastrointestinal infection, which was equally painful. The war would always affect him. Yet when his service was finished, he returned home and had to begin an entirely new life and career. OWH married and entered the legal world. Watson eventually married and continued as a physician, both learned professions. OWH wrote prodigiously and wrote well. Watson wrote an entire Canon of stories and created a legend.

For so many readers, it's not the plots or even the wording and style that matters. It's the sense of *identification* that draws our attention, elicits our fascination, and ensures our loyalty. So many Sherlockians have said that while they admire and revere Sherlock Holmes, it's John Watson whom we come to love and see as a friend and extension of our own simpler lives. The world often sees The Great Detective as Conan Doyle's greatest creation. But without Watson, would anyone remember or care about such "popular literature."

One can only wonder, but must indeed wonder, if it was really Watson, whose life was such a mirror here, whose journey and times caught the eye and the mind of Oliver. Without Watson, that greatest of unsung heroes, perhaps Oliver would have regarded Sherlock as just a "quick read" rather than a lifetime companion. We can speculate, but those who understand the Civil War and the Sherlockian Canon might understand how the Twentieth Massachusetts marched to Baker Street.

"A VERY SEEDY HARD FELT HAT."

What follows is a complete reproduction of the text
(by Arthur Conan Doyle) and illustrations (by Sidney Paget)
of "The Adventure of the Blue Carbuncle" as the story was first
printed in the January 1892 issue of The Strand Magazine.

THE ADVENTURE OF THE BLUE CARBUNCLE

ARTHUR CONAN DOYLE

I had called upon my friend Sherlock Holmes upon the second morning after Christmas, with the intention of wishing him the compliments of the season. He was lounging upon the sofa in a purple dressing-gown, a pipe-rack within his reach upon the right, and a pile of crumpled morning papers, evidently newly studied, near at hand. Beside the couch was a wooden chair, and on the angle of the back hung a very seedy and disreputable hard felt hat, much the worse for wear, and cracked in several places. A lens and a forceps lying upon the seat of the chair suggested that the hat had been suspended in this manner for the purpose of examination.

"You are engaged," said I; "perhaps I interrupt you."

"Not at all. I am glad to have a friend with whom I can discuss my results. The matter is a perfectly trivial one" (he jerked his thumb in the direction of the old hat), "but there are points in connection with it which are not entirely devoid of interest, and even of instruction."

I seated myself in his armchair, and warmed my hands before his crackling fire, for a sharp frost had set in, and the windows were thick with the ice crystals. "I suppose," I remarked, "that, homely as it looks, this thing has some deadly story linked on to it — that it is the clue which will guide you in the solution of some mystery, and the punishment of some crime."

"No, no. No crime," said Sherlock Holmes, laughing. "Only one of those whimsical little incidents which will happen when you have four million human beings all jostling each other within the space of a few square miles. Amid the action and reaction of so dense a swarm of humanity, every possible combination of events may be expected to take place, and many a little problem will be presented which may be striking and bizarre without being criminal. We have already had experience of such."

"So much so," I remarked, "that, of the last six cases which I have added to my notes, three have been entirely free of any legal crime."

"Precisely. You allude to my attempt to recover the Irene Adler papers, to the singular case of Miss Mary Sutherland, and to the adventure of the man with the twisted lip. Well, I have no doubt that this small matter will fall into the same innocent category. You know Peterson, the commissionaire?"

"Yes."

"It is to him that this trophy belongs."

"It is his hat."

"No, no; he found it. Its owner is unknown. I beg that you will look upon it, not as a battered billycock, but as an intellectual problem. And, first, as to how it came here. It arrived upon Christmas morning, in company with a good fat goose, which is, I have no doubt, roasting at this moment in front of Peterson's fire. The facts are these. About four o'clock on Christmas morning, Peterson, who, as you know, is a very honest fellow, was returning from some small jollification, and was making his way homewards down Tottenham Court-road. In front of him he saw, in the gaslight, a tallish man, walking with a slight stagger, and carrying a white goose slung over his shoulder. As he reached the corner of Goodge-street, a row broke out between this stranger and a little knot of roughs. One of the latter knocked off the man's hat, on which he raised his stick to defend himself, and, swinging it over his head, smashed the shop window behind him. Peterson had rushed forward to protect the stranger from his assailants, but the man, shocked at having broken the window, and seeing an official-looking person in uniform rushing towards him, dropped his goose, took to his heels, and vanished amid the labyrinth of small streets which lie at the back of Tottenham Court-road. The roughs had also fled at the appearance of Peterson, so that he was left in possession of the field of battle, and also of the spoils of victory in the shape of this battered hat and a most unimpeachable Christmas goose."

"Which surely he restored to their owner?"

"My dear fellow, there lies the problem. It is true that 'For Mrs. Henry Baker' was printed upon a small card which was tied to the bird's left leg, and it is also true that the initials 'H.B.' are legible upon the lining of this hat; but, as there are some thousands of Bakers, and some hundreds of Henry Bakers in this city of ours, it is not easy to restore lost property to any

"THE ROUGHS HAD FLED AT THE APPEARANCE OF PETERSON."

one of them."

"What, then, did Peterson do?"

"He brought round both hat and goose to me on Christmas morning, knowing that even the smallest problems are of interest to me. The goose we retained until this morning, when there were signs that, in spite of the slight frost, it would be well that it should be eaten without unnecessary delay. Its finder has carried it off, therefore, to fulfil the ultimate destiny of a goose, while I continue to retain the hat of the unknown gentleman who lost his Christmas dinner."

"Did he not advertise?"

"No."

"Then, what clue could you have as to his identity?"

"Only as much as we can deduce."

"From his hat?"

"Precisely."

"But you are joking. What can you gather from this old battered felt?"

"Here is my lens. You know my methods. What can you gather yourself as to the individuality of the man who has worn this article?"

I took the tattered object in my hands, and turned it over rather ruefully. It was a very ordinary black hat of the usual round shape, hard, and much the worse for wear. The lining had been of red silk, but was a good deal discoloured. There was no maker's name; but, as Holmes had remarked, the initials "H.B." were scrawled upon one side. It was pierced in the brim for a hat-securer, but the elastic was missing. For the rest, it was cracked, exceedingly dusty, and spotted in several places, although there seemed to have been some attempt to hide the discoloured patches by smearing them with ink.

"I can see nothing," said I, handing it back to my friend.

"On the contrary, Watson, you can see everything. You fail, however, to reason from what you see. You are too timid in drawing your inferences."

"Then, pray tell me what it is that you can infer from this hat?"

He picked it up, and gazed at it in the peculiar introspective fashion which was characteristic of him. "It is perhaps less suggestive than it might have been," he remarked, "and yet there are a few inferences which are very distinct, and a few others which represent at least a strong balance of probability. That the man was highly intellectual is of course obvious upon the face of it, and also that he was fairly well-to-do within the last three years, although he has now fallen upon evil days. He had foresight, but has less now than formerly, pointing to a moral retrogression, which, when taken with the decline of his fortunes, seems to indicate some evil influence, probably drink, at work upon him. This may account also for the obvious fact that his wife has ceased to love him."

"My dear Holmes!"

"He has, however, retained some degree of self-respect," he continued, disregarding my remonstrance. "He is a man who leads a sedentary life, goes out little, is out of training entirely, is middle-aged, has grizzled hair which he has had cut within the last few days, and which he anoints with lime-cream. These are the more patent facts which are to be deduced from his hat. Also, by the way, that it is extremely improbable that he has gas laid on in his house."

"You are certainly joking, Holmes."

"Not in the least. Is it possible that even now when I give you these results you are unable to see how they are attained?"

"I have no doubt that I am very stupid; but I must confess that I am unable to follow you. For example, how did you deduce that this man was intellectual?"

For answer Holmes clapped the hat upon his head. It came right over the forehead and settled upon the bridge of his nose. "It is a question of cubic capacity," said he; "a man with so large a brain must have something in it."

"The decline of his fortunes, then?"

"This hat is three years old. These flat brims curled at the edge came in then. It is a hat of the very best quality. Look at the band of ribbed silk, and the excellent lining. If this man could afford to buy so expensive a hat three years ago, and has had no hat since, then he has assuredly gone down in the world."

"Well, that is dear enough, certainly. But how about the foresight, and the moral retrogression?"

Sherlock Holmes laughed. "Here is the foresight," said he, putting his finger upon the little disc and loop of the hat-securer. "They are never sold upon hats. If this man ordered one, it is a sign of a certain amount of foresight, since he went out of his way to take this precaution against the wind. But since we see that he has broken the elastic, and has not troubled to replace it, it is obvious that he has less foresight now than formerly, which is a distinct proof of a weakening nature. On the other hand, he has endeavoured to conceal some of these stains upon the felt by daubing them with ink, which is a sign that he has not entirely lost his self-respect."

"Your reasoning is certainly plausible."

"The further points, that he is middle-aged, that his hair is grizzled, that it has been recently cut, and that he uses lime-cream, are all to be gathered from a close examination of the lower part of the lining. The lens discloses a large number of hair ends, clean cut by the scissors of the barber. They all appear to be adhesive, and there is a distinct odour of lime-cream. This dust, you will observe, is not the gritty, grey dust of the street, but the fluffy brown dust of the house, showing that it has been hung up indoors most of the time; while the marks of moisture upon the inside are proof positive that the wearer perspired very freely, and could, therefore, hardly be in the best of training."

"But his wife — you said that she had ceased to love him."

"This hat has not been brushed for weeks. When I see you, my dear Watson, with a week's accumulation of dust upon your hat, and when your wife allows you to go out in such a state, I shall fear that you also have been unfortunate enough to lose your wife's affection."

"But he might be a bachelor."

"Nay, he was bringing home the goose as a peace offering to his wife. Remember the card upon the bird's leg."

"You have an answer to everything. But how on earth do you deduce that the gas is not laid on in the house?"

"One tallow stain, or even two, might come by chance; but, when I see no less than five, I think that there can be little doubt that the individual must be brought into frequent contact with burning tallow — walks upstairs at night probably with his hat in one hand and a guttering candle in the other. Anyhow, he never got tallow stains from a gas jet. Are you satisfied?"

"Well, it is very ingenious," said I, laughing; "but, since, as you said just now, there has been no crime committed, and no harm done save the loss of a goose, all this seems to be rather a waste of energy."

Sherlock Holmes had opened his mouth to reply, when the door flew open, and Peterson the commissionaire rushed into

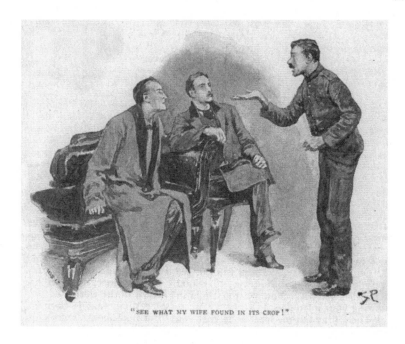

"SEE WHAT MY WIFE FOUND IN ITS CROP!"

the compartment with flushed cheeks and the face of a man who is dazed with astonishment.

"The goose, Mr. Holmes! The goose, sir!" he gasped.

"Eh? What of it, then? Has it returned to life, and flapped off through the kitchen window?" Holmes twisted himself round upon the sofa to get a fairer view of the man's excited face.

"See here, sir! See what my wife found in its crop!" He held out his hand, and displayed upon the centre of the palm a brilliantly scintillating blue stone, rather smaller than a bean in size, but of such purity and radiance that it twinkled like an electric point in the dark hollow of his hand.

Sherlock Holmes sat up with a whistle. "By Jove, Peterson!" said he, "this is treasure trove indeed! I suppose you know what you have got?"

"A diamond, sir! A precious stone! It cuts into glass as though it were putty."

"It's more than a precious stone. It's *the* precious stone."

"Not the Countess of Morcar's blue carbuncle?" I ejaculated.

"Precisely so. I ought to know its size and shape, seeing that I have read the advertisement about it in *The Times* every day lately. It is absolutely unique, and its value can only be conjectured, but the reward offered of a thousand pounds is certainly not within a twentieth part of the market price."

"A thousand pounds! Great Lord of mercy!" The commissionaire plumped down into a chair, and stared from one to the other of us.

"That is the reward, and I have reason to know that there are sentimental considerations in the background which would induce the Countess to part with half of her fortune, if she could but recover the gem."

"It was lost, if I remember aright, at the Hotel Cosmopolitan," I remarked.

"Precisely so, on the twenty-second of December, just five days ago. John Horner, a plumber, was accused of having abstracted it from the lady's jewel case. The evidence against him was so strong that the case has been referred to the Assizes. I have some account of the matter here, I believe." He rummaged amid his newspapers, glancing over the dates, until at last he smoothed one out, doubled it over, and read the following paragraph:—

"Hotel Cosmopolitan Jewel Robbery. John Horner, 26, plumber, was brought up upon the charge of having upon the

22nd inst. abstracted from the jewel case of the Countess of Morcar the valuable gem known as the blue carbuncle. James Ryder, upper-attendant at the hotel, gave his evidence to the effect that he had shown Horner up to the dressing-room of the Countess of Morcar upon the day of the robbery, in order that he might solder the second bar of the grate, which was loose. He had remained with Horner some little time, but had finally been called away. On returning, he found that Horner had disappeared, that the bureau had been forced open, and that the small morocco casket in which, as it afterwards transpired, the Countess was accustomed to keep her jewel, was lying empty upon the dressing-table. Ryder instantly gave the alarm, and Horner was arrested the same evening; but the stone could not be found either upon his person or in his rooms. Catherine Cusack, maid to the Countess, deposed to having heard Ryder's cry of dismay on discovering the robbery, and to having rushed into the room, where she found matters were as described by the last witness. Inspector Bradstreet, B division, gave evidence as to the arrest of Horner, who struggled frantically, and protested his innocence in the strongest terms. Evidence of a previous conviction for robbery having been given against the prisoner, the magistrate refused to deal summarily with the offence, but referred it to the Assizes. Horner, who had shown signs of intense emotion during the proceedings, fainted away at the conclusion, and was carried out of court."

"Hum! So much for the police-court," said Holmes, thoughtfully, tossing aside the paper. "The question for us now to solve is the sequence of events leading from a rifled jewel case at one end to the crop of a goose in Tottenham Court-road at the other. You see, Watson, our little deductions have suddenly assumed a much more important and less innocent aspect. Here is the stone; the stone came from the goose, and the goose came from Mr. Henry Baker, the gentleman with the bad hat and all the other characteristics with which I have bored you. So now we must set ourselves very seriously to finding this gentleman, and ascertaining what part he has played in this little mystery. To do this, we must try the simplest means first, and these lie undoubtedly in an advertisement in all the evening papers. If this fail, I shall have recourse to other methods."

"What will you say?"

"Give me a pencil, and that slip of paper. Now, then: 'Found at the corner of Goodge-street, a goose and a black felt hat. Mr. Henry Baker can have the same by applying at 6.30 this evening at 221B Baker-street.' That is clear and concise."

"Very. But will he see it?"

"Well, he is sure to keep an eye on the papers, since, to a poor man, the loss was a heavy one. He was clearly so scared by his mischance in breaking the window, and by the approach of Peterson, that he thought of nothing but flight; but since then he must have bitterly regretted the impulse which caused him to drop his bird. Then, again, the introduction of his name will cause him to see it, for everyone who knows him will direct his attention to it. Here you are, Peterson, run down to the advertising agency, and have this put in the evening papers."

"In which, sir."

"Oh, in the *Globe, Star, Pall Mall, St. James's, Evening News, Standard, Echo,* and any others that occur to you."

"Very well, sir. And this stone?"

"Ah, yes, I shall keep the stone. Thank you. And, I say, Peterson, just buy a goose on your way back, and leave it here with me, for we must have one to give to this gentleman in place of the one which your family is now devouring."

When the commissionaire had gone, Holmes took up the stone and held it against the light. "It's a bonny thing," said he. "Just see how it glints and sparkles. Of course it is a nucleus and focus of crime. Every good stone is. They are the devil's pet baits. In the larger and older jewels every facet may stand for a bloody deed. This stone is not yet twenty years old. It was found in the banks of the Amoy River in Southern China, and is remarkable in having every characteristic of the carbuncle, save that it is blue in shade, instead of ruby red. In spite of its youth, it has already a sinister history. There have been two murders, a vitriol-throwing, a suicide, and several robberies brought about for the sake of this forty-grain weight of crystallised charcoal. Who would think that so pretty a toy would be a purveyor to the gallows and the prison? I'll lock it up in my strong box now, and drop a line to the Countess to say that we have it."

"Do you think this man Horner is innocent?"

"I cannot tell."

"Well, then, do you imagine that this other one, Henry Baker, had anything to do with the matter?"

"It is, I think, much more likely that Henry Baker is an

absolutely innocent man, who had no idea that the bird which he was carrying was of considerably more value than if it were made of solid gold. That, however, I shall determine by a very simple test, if we have an answer to our advertisement."

"And you can do nothing until then?"

"Nothing."

"In that case I shall continue my professional round. But I shall come back in the evening at the hour you have mentioned, for I should like to see the solution of so tangled a business."

"Very glad to see you. I dine at seven. There is a woodcock, I believe. By the way, in view of recent occurrences, perhaps I ought to ask Mrs. Hudson to examine its crop."

I had been delayed at a case, and it was a little after half-past six when I found myself in Baker-street once more. As I approached the house I saw a tall man in a Scotch bonnet, with a coat which was buttoned up to his chin, waiting outside in the bright semicircle which was thrown from the fanlight. Just as I arrived, the door was opened, and we were shown up together to Holmes' room.

"Mr. Henry Baker, I believe," said he, rising from his armchair, and greeting his visitor with the easy air of geniality which he could so readily assume. "Pray take this chair by the fire, Mr. Baker. It is a cold night, and I observe that your circulation is more adapted for summer than for winter. Ah, Watson, you have just come at the right time. Is that your hat, Mr. Baker?"

"Yes, sir, that is undoubtedly my hat."

He was a large man, with rounded shoulders, a massive head,

and a broad, intelligent face, sloping down to a pointed beard of grizzled brown. A touch of red in nose and cheeks, with a slight tremor of his extended hand, recalled Holmes' surmise as to his habits. His rusty black frock coat was buttoned right up in front, with the collar turned up, and his lank wrists protruded from his sleeves without a sign of cuff or shirt. He spoke in a slow staccato fashion, choosing his words with care, and gave the impression generally of a man of learning and letters who had had ill-usage at the hands of fortune.

"We have retained these things for some days," said Holmes, "because we expected to see an advertisement from you giving your address. I am at a loss to know now why you did not advertise."

Our visitor gave a rather shame-faced laugh. "Shillings have not been so plentiful with me as they once were," he remarked. "I had no doubt that the gang of roughs who assaulted me had carried off both my hat and the bird. I did not care to spend more money in a hopeless attempt at recovering them."

"Very naturally. By the way, about the bird, we were compelled to eat it."

"To eat it!" Our visitor half rose from his chair in his excitement.

"Yes, it would have been no use to anyone had we not done so. But I presume that this other goose upon the sideboard, which is about the same weight and perfectly fresh, will answer your purpose equally well?"

"Oh, certainly, certainly!" answered Mr. Baker, with a sigh of relief.

"Of course, we still have the feathers, legs, crop, and so on of your own bird, if you so wish —"

The man burst into a hearty laugh. "They might be useful to me as relics of my adventure," said he, "but beyond that I can hardly see what use the *disjecta membra* of my late acquaintance are going to be to me. No, sir, I think that, with your permission, I will confine my attentions to the excellent bird which I perceive upon the sideboard."

Sherlock Holmes glanced sharply across at me with a slight shrug of his shoulders.

"There is your hat, then, and there your bird," said he. "By the way, would it bore you to tell me where you got the other one from? I am somewhat of a fowl fancier, and I have seldom seen a better-grown goose."

"Certainly, sir," said Baker, who had risen and tucked his newly-gained property under his arm. "There are a few of us who frequent the 'Alpha' Inn, near the Museum — we are to be found in the Museum itself during the day, you understand. This year our good host, Windigate by name, instituted a goose club, by which, on consideration of some few pence every week, we were to receive a bird at Christmas. My pence were duly paid, and the rest is familiar to you. I am much indebted to you, sir, for a Scotch bonnet is fitted neither to my years nor my gravity." With a comical pomposity of manner he bowed solemnly to both of us, and strode off upon his way.

"So much for Mr. Henry Baker," said Holmes, when he had closed the door behind him. "It is quite certain that he knows nothing whatever about the matter. Are you hungry, Watson?"

"HE BOWED SOLEMNLY TO BOTH OF US."

"Not particularly."

"Then I suggest that we turn our dinner into a supper, and follow up this clue while it is still hot."

"By all means."

It was a bitter night, so we drew on our ulsters and wrapped cravats about our throats. Outside, the stars were shining coldly in a cloudless sky, and the breath of the passers-by blew out into smoke like so many pistol shots. Our footfalls rang out crisply and loudly as we swung through the Doctors' quarter, Wimpole-street, Harley-street, and so through Wigmore-street into Oxford-street. In a quarter of an hour we were in Bloomsbury at the "Alpha" Inn, which is a small public-house at the corner of one of the streets which run down into Holborn. Holmes pushed open the door of the private bar, and ordered two glasses of beer from the ruddy-faced, white-aproned landlord.

"Your beer should be excellent if it is as good as your geese," he said.

"My geese!" The man seemed surprised.

"Yes. I was speaking only half an hour ago to Mr. Henry Baker, who was a member of your goose-club."

"Ah! yes, I see. But you see, sir, them's not *our* geese."

"Indeed! Whose, then?"

"Well, I got the two dozen from a salesman in Covent Garden."

"Indeed! I know some of them. Which was it?"

"Breckinridge is his name."

"Ah! I don't know him. Well, here's your good health, landlord, and prosperity to your house. Good-night!"

"Now for Mr. Breckinridge," he continued, buttoning up his coat, as we came out into the frosty air. "Remember, Watson, that though we have so homely a thing as a goose at one end of this chain, we have at the other a man who will certainly get seven years' penal servitude, unless we can establish his innocence. It is possible that our inquiry may but confirm his guilt; but, in any case, we have a line of investigation which has been missed by the police, and which a singular chance has placed in our hands. Let us follow it out to the bitter end. Faces to the south, then, and quick march!"

We passed across Holborn, down Endell-street, and so through a zigzag of slums to Covent Garden Market. One of the largest stalls bore the name of Breckinridge upon it, and the proprietor, a horsey-looking man, with a sharp face and trim side-whiskers, was helping a boy to put up the shutters.

"Good evening. It's a cold night," said Holmes.

The salesman nodded, and shot a questioning glance at my companion.

"Sold out of geese, I see," continued Holmes, pointing at the bare slabs of marble.

"Let you have five hundred to-morrow morning."

"That's no good."

"Well, there are some on the stall with the gas flare."

"Ah, but I was recommended to you."

"Who by?"

"The landlord of the 'Alpha.'"

"Oh, yes; I sent him a couple of dozen."

"Fine birds they were, too. Now where did you get them from?"

To my surprise the question provoked a burst of anger from the salesman.

"Now, then, mister," said he, with his head cocked and his arms akimbo, "what are you driving at? Let's have it straight, now."

"It is straight enough. I should like to know who sold you

the geese which you supplied to the 'Alpha.'"

"Well, then, I sha'n't tell you. So now!"

"Oh, it is a matter of no importance; but I don't know why you should be so warm over such a trifle."

"Warm! You'd be as warm, maybe, if you were as pestered as I am. When I pay good money for a good article there should be an end to the business; but it's 'Where are the geese?' and 'Who did you sell the geese to?' and 'What will you take for the geese?' One would think they were the only geese in the world, to hear the fuss that is made over them."

"Well, I have no connection with any other people who have been making inquiries," said Holmes carelessly. "If you won't tell us the bet is off, that is all. But I'm always ready to back my opinion on a matter of fowls, and I have a fiver on it that the bird I ate is country bred."

"Well, then, you've lost your fiver, for it's town bred," snapped the salesman.

"It's nothing of the kind."

"I say it is."

"I don't believe it."

"D'you think you know more about fowls than I, who have handled them ever since I was a nipper? I tell you, all those birds that went to the 'Alpha' were town bred."

"You'll never persuade me to believe that."

"Will you bet, then?"

"It's merely taking your money, for I know that I am right. But I'll have a sovereign on with you, just to teach you not to be obstinate."

The salesman chuckled grimly. "Bring me the books, Bill," said he.

The small boy brought round a small thin volume and a great greasy-backed one, laying them out together beneath the hanging lamp.

"Now then, Mr. Cocksure," said the salesman, "I thought that I was out of geese, but before I finish you'll find that there is still one left in my shop. You see this little book?"

"Well?"

"That's the list of the folk from whom I buy. D'you see? Well, then, here on this page are the country folk, and the numbers after their names are where their accounts are in the big ledger. Now, then! You see this other page in red ink? Well, that is a list of my town suppliers. Now, look at that third name. Just read it out to me."

"Mrs. Oakshott, 117, Brixton-road — 249," read Holmes.

"Quite so. Now turn that up in the ledger."

Holmes turned to the page indicated. "Here you are, 'Mrs. Oakshott, 117, Brixton-road, egg and poultry supplier.'"

"Now, then, what's the last entry?"

"'December 22. Twenty-four geese at 7s. 6d.'"

"Quite so. There you are. And underneath?"

"'Sold to Mr. Windigate of the 'Alpha' at 12s.'"

"What have you to say now?"

Sherlock Holmes looked deeply chagrined. He drew a sovereign from his pocket and threw it down upon the slab, turning away with the air of a man whose disgust is too deep for words. A few yards off he stopped under a lamp-

"JUST READ IT OUT TO ME."

post, and laughed in the hearty, noiseless fashion which was peculiar to him.

"When you see a man with whiskers of that cut and the 'Pink 'un' protruding out of his pocket, you can always draw him by a bet," said he. "I daresay that if I had put a hundred pounds down in front of him that man would not have given me such complete information as was drawn from him by the idea that he was doing me on a wager. Well, Watson, we are, I fancy, nearing the end of our quest, and the only point which remains to be determined is whether we should go on to this Mrs. Oakshott to-night, or whether we should reserve it for to-morrow. It is clear from what that surly fellow said that there are others besides ourselves who are anxious about the matter, and I should —"

His remarks were suddenly cut short by a loud hubbub which broke out from the stall which we had just left. Turning round we saw a little rat-faced fellow standing in the centre of the circle of yellow light which was thrown by the swinging lamp, while Breckinridge the salesman, framed in the door of his stall, was shaking his fists fiercely at the cringing figure.

"I've had enough of you and your geese," he shouted. "I wish you were all at the devil together. If you come pestering me any more with your silly talk I'll set the dog at you. You bring Mrs. Oakshott here and I'll answer her, but what have you to do with it? Did I buy the geese off you?"

"No; but one of them was mine all the same," whined the little man.

"Well, then, ask Mrs. Oakshott for it."

"She told me to ask you."

"Well, you can ask the King of Proosia for all I care. I've had enough of it. Get out of this!" He rushed fiercely forward, and the inquirer flitted away into the darkness.

"Ha, this may save us a visit to Brixton-road," whispered Holmes. "Come with me, and we will see what is to be made of this fellow." Striding through the scattered knots of people who lounged round the flaring stalls, my companion speedily overtook the little man and touched him upon the shoulder. He sprang round, and I could see in the gaslight that every vestige of colour had been driven from his face.

"Who are you, then? What do you want?" he asked in a quavering voice.

"You will excuse me," said Holmes blandly, "but I could not

help overhearing the questions which you put to the salesman
just now. I think that I could be of assistance to you."

"You? Who are you? How could you know anything of the
matter?"

"My name is Sherlock Holmes. It is my business to know
what other people don't know."

"But you can know nothing of this?"

"Excuse me, I know everything of it. You are endeavouring
to trace some geese which were sold by Mrs. Oakshott, of
Brixton Road, to a salesman named Breckinridge, by him in
turn to Mr. Windigate, of the 'Alpha,' and by him to his club,
of which Mr. Henry Baker is a member."

"Oh, sir, you are the very man whom I have longed to meet,"
cried the little fellow, with outstretched hands and quivering
fingers. "I can hardly explain to you how interested I am in
this matter."

Sherlock Holmes hailed a four-wheeler which was passing.
"In that case we had better discuss it in a cosy room rather
than in this windswept market-place," said he. "But pray tell
me, before we go further, who it is that I have the pleasure
of assisting."

The man hesitated for an instant. "My name is John
Robinson," he answered, with a sidelong glance.

"No, no; the real name," said Holmes sweetly. "It is always
awkward doing business with an *alias*."

A flush sprang to the white cheeks of the stranger. "Well,
then," said he, "my real name is James Ryder."

"Precisely so. Head attendant at the Hotel Cosmopolitan.

"YOU ARE THE VERY MAN."

Pray step into the cab, and I shall soon be able to tell you everything which you would wish to know."

The little man stood glancing from one to the other of us with half-frightened, half-hopeful eyes, as one who is not sure whether he is on the verge of a windfall or of a catastrophe. Then he stepped into the cab, and in half an hour we were back in the sitting-room at Baker-street. Nothing had been said during our drive, but the high thin breathing of our new companion, and the claspings and unclaspings of his hands spoke of the nervous tension within him.

"Here we are!" said Holmes, cheerily, as we filed into the room. "The fire looks very seasonable in this weather. You look cold, Mr. Ryder. Pray take the basket chair. I will just put on my slippers before we settle this little matter of yours. Now, then! You want to know what became of those geese?"

"Yes, sir."

"Or rather, I fancy, of that goose. It was one bird, I imagine, in which you were interested — white, with a black bar across the tail."

Ryder quivered with emotion. "Oh, sir," he cried, "can you tell me where it went to?"

"It came here."

"Here?"

"Yes, and a most remarkable bird it proved. I don't wonder that you should take an interest in it. It laid an egg after it was dead — the bonniest, brightest little blue egg that ever was seen. I have it here in my museum."

Our visitor staggered to his feet, and clutched the mantelpiece with his right hand. Holmes unlocked his strong box, and held up the blue carbuncle, which shone out like a star, with a cold, brilliant, many-pointed radiance. Ryder stood glaring with a drawn face, uncertain whether to claim or to disown it.

"The game's up, Ryder," said Holmes quietly. "Hold up,

man, or you'll be into the fire. Give him an arm back into his chair, Watson. He's not got blood enough to go in for felony with impunity. Give him a dash of brandy. So! Now he looks a little more human. What a shrimp it is, to be sure!"

For a moment he had staggered and nearly fallen, but the brandy brought a tinge of colour into his cheeks, and he sat staring with frightened eyes at his accuser.

"I have almost every link in my hands, and all the proofs which I could possibly need, so there is little which you need tell me. Still that little may as well be cleared up to make the case complete. You had heard, Ryder, of this blue stone of the Countess of Morcar's?"

"It was Catherine Cusack who told me of it," said he, in a crackling voice.

"I see. Her ladyship's waiting maid. Well, the temptation of sudden wealth so easily acquired was too much for you, as it has been for better men before you; but you were not very scrupulous in the means you used. It seems to me, Ryder, that there is the making of a very pretty villain in you. You knew that this man Horner, the plumber, had been concerned in some such matter before, and that suspicion would rest the more readily upon him. What did you do, then? You made some small job in my lady's room — you and your confederate Cusack — and you managed that he should be the man sent for. Then, when he had left, you rifled the jewel case, raised the alarm, and had this unfortunate man arrested. You then —"

Ryder threw himself down suddenly upon the rug, and clutched at my companion's knees. "For God's sake, have

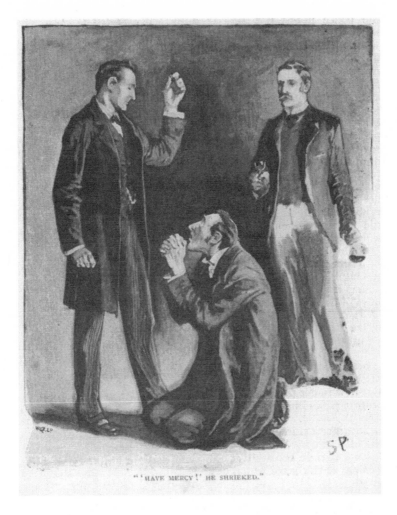

"'HAVE MERCY!' HE SHRIEKED."

mercy!" he shrieked. "Think of my father! Of my mother! It would break their hearts. I never went wrong before! I never will again. I swear it. I'll swear it on a Bible. Oh, don't bring it into court! For Christ's sake, don't!"

"Get back into your chair!" said Holmes sternly. "It is very well to cringe and crawl now, but you thought little enough of this poor Horner in the dock for a crime of which he knew nothing."

"I will fly, Mr. Holmes. I will leave the country, sir. Then the charge against him will break down."

"Hum! We will talk about that. And now let us hear a true account of the next act. How came the stone into the goose, and how came the goose into the open market? Tell us the truth, for there lies your only hope of safety."

Ryder passed his tongue over his parched lips. "I will tell you it just as it happened, sir," said he. "When Horner had been arrested, it seemed to me that it would be best for me to get away with the stone at once, for I did not know at what moment the police might not take it into their heads to search me and my room. There was no place about the hotel where it would be safe. I went out, as if on some commission, and I made for my sister's house. She had married a man named Oakshott, and lived in Brixton-road, where she fattened fowls for the market. All the way there every man I met seemed to me to be a policeman or a detective, and for all that it was a cold night, the sweat was pouring down my face before I came to the Brixton-road. My sister asked me what was the matter, and why I was so pale; but I told her that I had been upset by the jewel robbery at the hotel. Then I went into the back yard, and smoked a pipe, and wondered what it would be best to do.

"I had a friend once called Maudsley, who went to the bad, and has just been serving his time in Pentonville. One day he had met me, and fell into talk about the ways of thieves and how they could get rid of what they stole. I knew that he would be true to me, for I knew one or two things about him, so I made up my mind to go right on to Kilburn, where he lived, and take him into my confidence. He would show me how to turn the stone into money. But how to get to him in safety? I thought of the agonies I had gone through in coming from the hotel. I might at any moment be seized and searched, and there would be the stone in my waistcoat pocket. I was leaning against the wall at the time, and looking at the geese which were waddling about round my feet, and suddenly an idea came into my head which showed me how I could beat the best detective that ever lived.

"My sister had told me some weeks before that I might have the pick of her geese for a Christmas present, and I knew that she was always as good as her word. I would take my goose now, and in it I would carry my stone to Kilburn. There was a little shed in the yard, and behind this I drove one of the birds, a fine big one, white, with a barred tail. I caught it, and, prizing its bill open, I thrust the stone down its throat as far as my finger could reach. The bird gave a gulp, and I felt the stone pass along its gullet and down into its crop. But the creature flapped and struggled, and out came my sister to know what was the matter. As I turned to speak to her the brute broke loose, and fluttered off among the others.

"'Whatever were you doing with that bird, Jem?' says she.

"'Well,' said I, 'you said you'd give me one for Christmas, and I was feeling which was the fattest.'

"'Oh,' says she, 'we've set yours aside for you. Jem's bird, we call it. It's the big, white one over yonder. There's twenty-six of them, which makes one for you, and one for us, and two dozen for the market.'

"'Thank you, Maggie,' says I; 'but if it is all the same to you I'd rather have that one I was handling just now.'

"'The other is a good three pound heavier,' she said, 'and we fattened it expressly for you.'

"'Never mind. I'll have the other, and I'll take it now,'" said I.

"'Oh, just as you like,' said she, a little huffed. 'Which is it you want, then?'

"'That white one, with the barred tail, right in the middle of the flock.'

"'Oh, very well. Kill it and take it with you.'

"Well, I did what she said, Mr. Holmes, and I carried the bird all the way to Kilburn. I told my pal what I had done, for he was a man that it was easy to tell a thing like that to. He laughed until he choked, and we got a knife and opened the goose. My heart turned to water, for there was no sign of the stone, and I knew that some terrible mistake had occurred. I left the bird, rushed back to my sister's, and hurried into the back yard. There was not a bird to be seen there.

"'Where are they all, Maggie?' I cried.

"'Gone to the dealer's, Jim.'

"'Which dealer's?'

"'Breckinridge, of Covent Garden.'

"'But was there another with a barred tail?' I asked, 'the same as the one I chose?'

"'Yes, Jem, there were two barred-tailed ones, and I could

never tell them apart.'

"Well, then, of course, I saw it all, and I ran off as hard as
my feet would carry me to this man Breckinridge; but he had
sold the lot at once, and not one word would he tell me as
to where they had gone. You heard him yourselves to-night.
Well, he has always answered me like that. My sister thinks
that I am going mad. Sometimes I think that I am myself. And
now — and now I am myself a branded thief, without ever
having touched the wealth for which I sold my character. God
help me! God help me!" He burst into convulsive sobbing,
with his face buried in his hands.

There was a long silence, broken only by his heavy
breathing, and by the measured tapping of Sherlock Holmes'
finger-tips upon the edge of the table. Then my friend rose,
and threw open the door.

"Get out!" said he.

"What, sir! Oh, heaven bless you!"

"No more words. Get out!"

And no more words were needed. There was a rush, a
clatter upon the stairs, the bang of a door, and the crisp rattle
of running footfalls from the street.

"After all, Watson," said Holmes, reaching up his hand for
his clay pipe, "I am not retained by the police to supply their
deficiencies. If Horner were in danger it would be another
thing, but this fellow will not appear against him, and the
case must collapse. I suppose that I am commuting a felony,
but it is just possible that I am saving a soul. This fellow will
not go wrong again. He is too terribly frightened. Send him

" HE BURST INTO CONVULSIVE SOBBING."

to gaol now, and you make him a gaol-bird for life. Besides, it is the season of forgiveness. Chance has put in our way a most singular and whimsical problem, and its solution is its own reward. If you will have the goodness to touch the bell, Doctor, we will begin another investigation, in which also a bird will be the chief feature."

CONTRIBUTORS

ROSS E. DAVIES is a professor of law at George Mason University and editor-in-chief of *The Green Bag*.

M.H. HOEFLICH is John H. & John M. Kane Distinguished Professor of Law at the University of Kansas School of Law.

ROBERT S. KATZ is a physician specializing in pathology and co-publisher of the Baker Street Irregulars Press.

CREDITS

Cover: Illustration by Sidney Paget. This is Paget's original work — now in the collection of Michael F. Whelan and Mary Ann Bradley — from which an etching was made to illustrate the first printing of "The Hound of the Baskervilles," in *The Strand Magazine*, Apr. 1902, page 368. It is reproduced here with the kind permission of the owners. The Sidney Paget illustration used on the front cover of this book is a proprietary version scanned directly from the original artwork and licensed exclusively from Wessex Press, LLC.

Frontispieces: Arthur Conan Doyle. Library of Congress Prints and Photographs Division, repro. no. LC-DIG-ggbain-34026 (n.d.). Oliver Wendell Holmes. Library of Congress Prints and Photographs Division, repro. no. LC-DIG-npcc-26413 (ca. 1924).

Page 16: Oliver Wendell Holmes. Library of Congress Prints and Photographs Division, repro. no. LC-DIG-bellcm-25712 (ca. 1890).

Page 26: Oliver Wendell Holmes. Library of Congress Prints and Photographs Division, repro. no. LC-DIG-npcc-27533 (Mar. 8, 1926).

Page 33: Charles Evans Hughes and Oliver Wendell Holmes. Library of Congress Prints and Photographs Division, repro. no. LC-DIG-hec-36289 (1931).

Page 34: Cartoon. *Life*, July 11, 1918, at 100.

Page 42: Oliver Wendell Holmes. Library of Congress Prints and Photographs Division, repro. no. LC-DIG-ppmsca-49594 (ca. 1862).

Pages 50-83: Illustrations by Sidney Paget, from the first printing of "The Adventure of the Blue Carbuncle," in *The Strand Magazine*, Jan. 1892, pages 73-85.